BLACK MONDAY

A crash that shook the financial world

Written by Patrice Moine
Translated by Rebecca Neal

BLACK MONDAY

A CRASH THAT SHOOK THE FINANCIAL WORLD

- **When:** 19 October 1987.
- **Where:** the New York Stock Exchange.
- **Context:** against a backdrop of rampant speculation, the unexpected announcement of the US trade deficit seriously worried investors and drove share prices down.
- **Key protagonists:**
  - Ronald Reagan (1911-2004), 40th President of the United States, 1981-1989. When Reagan came into office in January 1981, he embarked on a programme of tax reduction in order to stimulate economic growth. As a result, stock markets around the world rose constantly during his presidency.
  - Paul Volcker (born in 1927), American economist and Chairman of the Federal Reserve from 1979 to 1987. He counte-

red inflation by raising exchange rates on the Federal Reserve.
  ◦ Alan Greenspan (born in 1926), American economist and Chairman of the Federal Reserve from 1987 to 2006. He supported banks during the darkest days of the 1987 crisis by supplying liquidity.

- **Key terms:**
  ◦ <u>Dow Jones</u>: the Dow Jones was created in 1885 and is the second-oldest stock exchange index in the United States. Even though it only lists 30 companies, it is a key reference point for the New York Stock Exchange.
  ◦ <u>Trading</u>: the buying or selling of shares on the financial markets, carried out by financial operators known as traders.
  ◦ <u>Speculation</u>: a risky financial operation which involves anticipating fluctuations on the market and buying a commodity with the aim of later reselling it at a profit.
  ◦ <u>Black Monday</u>: the day when the Dow Jones lost 22.6% of its value, the largest drop ever recorded on the New York Stock Exchange.

The Wall Street Crash of 1929, with the famous Black Thursday on 24 October, hit the New York Stock Exchange and plunged the country into the Great Depression, before spreading across the world. It went down in history as the worst financial crisis of the 20th century, and now holds an important place in collective memory.

Almost 58 years to the day after this crisis, the world of finance was hit by another crash. While the world was enjoying a period of relative economic prosperity, panic spread through the New York Stock Exchange on Monday 19 October 1987: so many orders were placed that the computers struggled to keep up, share prices collapsed and the Dow Jones dropped by 22.6% in the space of a single day.

This crash on the world's leading stock exchange had a knock-on effect around the world. The main stock markets were soon thrown into disarray, losing an average of 25% of their value on 19 October alone:

- the Hong Kong stock market was closed for a week to deal with the fallout from a 45% drop in value at the end of October;

- the London stock market lost 26% of its value;
- the Sydney stock market lost 25% of its value;
- the Toronto stock market lost 22% of its value;
- the Tokyo stock market lost 15% of its value;
- the Paris stock market "only" lost 9% of its value, but continued to decline for several days afterwards.

The financial sector was taken by surprise by the crash because it was so unexpected: since 1982, the American market had enjoyed sustained growth and was experiencing a period of prosperity, meaning that it could be labelled a bull market (a market where share prices are constantly increasing). Investor confidence reached euphoric heights, and this widespread elation made anything seem possible. However, the financial markets gradually lost sight of the real economy in favour of speculation, which ultimately led to the sector's downfall.

In the end, the fall in share prices was twice as large in terms of percentage as the Wall Street Crash in 1929, but fortunately its consequences were far less tragic for the real economy.

THE WORST FINANCIAL CRISES IN HISTORY

- On 24 October 1929, known as Black Thursday, the famous **Wall Street Crash** took place. The following Monday, the Dow Jones lost 13% of its value, and it declined even further over the course of the following days.
- 19 October 1987 became known as **Black Monday**, as the Dow Jones lost over 22% of its value (thus surpassing the losses of the Wall Street Crash in 1929), which led to major slumps in stock markets around the world.
- In March 2000, the **burst of the dot-com bubble** resulting from excessive speculation on internet companies caused the Nasdaq stock market index (which lists companies with high growth potential, particularly in the cutting-edge technology sector) to fall by 27% in the space of two weeks.
- In 2008, the **subprime mortgage crisis** in the USA, linked to defaults on risky mortgages, led to international markets collapsing by over 30%.

CONTEXT

THE RESURGENCE OF THE STOCK MARKETS

Trading rooms

Trading rooms first appeared in the late 1970s and came to Europe in 1982, with the bank Indosuez's trading room in Paris. These are open-plan offices where trading and financial investment teams work. As well as operators on the different markets, financial engineers and IT specialists also work there.

Trading rooms can be very large: for example, that of the Swiss financial services company UBS has an area of 10 000 m^2 and features 1400 workspaces and 5000 screens.

The development of trading rooms went hand in hand with the development of microcomputers and workstations (supercomputers which run multi-user operating systems). These tools allowed data to be processed much more quickly and in far larger quantities, which drastically changed trading.

Computer trading

In the period leading up to the crash, information technology developed enough to make computer trading, meaning trading carried out automatically by computers, possible. There was little regulation covering the effects of these new tools, and they undoubtedly played a part in the burgeoning crisis, although they were not its sole cause.

Two major changes revolutionised the technical operation of financial centres:

- computerisation, as more and more work was done by computers;
- the shift to paperless trading, which allowed orders to be placed in real time.

Decisions about the buying and selling of transferable securities then became immediate and automatic. Computers used pre-established, programmed models of behaviour to make decisions about buying and selling shares and to place stock exchange orders immediately.

Computers can decide on and place orders in real time, work with volumes that would be impossible for humans, and eliminate all feelings and hesitation. On the other hand, they are automata and lack intuition and experience, which are both essential in stock market trading.

The Paris Bourse

Until 1987, the Paris Bourse was located at the Palais Brongniart and transactions were still carried out through open outcry. That year marked the end of an era, as shares were no longer listed on the red velvet-carpeted balustrade of the Palais Brongniart and traded by official stockbrokers known as *agents de change*, who held a legal monopoly on trading.

From this point onwards, the Bourse became computerised and the CAC (Cotation Assistée en Continu, or Continuous Assisted Quotation) system was introduced. One year later, the legal monopoly held by the *agents de change* also came to an end, and they were replaced by the Société des bourses françaises (Society of French

Stock Markets).

Until November 1984, equities and their owners were shown on a document representing a part of the capital of the listed companies, with little rectangles serving as coupons authorising the (possible) payment of dividends. These documents belonged "to the bearer"; in other words, to the person holding them.

After this date, book entries replaced the system of shares on paper. Euroclear France SA managed all the shares in circulation, which increased market fluidity. The stock exchange went online, which made high-volume trading possible.

EFFORTS TO STABILISE EXCHANGE RATES

Starting in 1982, and particularly because of this technological progress, the main stock markets around the world enjoyed a remarkable period of growth, leaving traders feeling euphoric. During this period, the value of the Paris stock market rose by 330%, that of London by 250%, and that of New York by 190%.

However, the picture was not entirely rosy. In June 1981 in the USA, Paul Volcker, the Chairman of the Federal Reserve (the institution in charge of American monetary policy) since 1979, appointed by Jimmy Carter (born in 1924) and confirmed by Reagan, decided to raise the federal funds rate in order to combat inflation, which had reached worrying proportions.

As a consequence, the value of the dollar rose for several years, supporting the American leaders' belief that a strong dollar illustrated the rest of the world's confidence in their economy, as well as their belief in the benefits of allowing the markets to dictate the exchange rate. However, although this strong dollar kept inflation under control, it also slowed down economic growth. Investment had become less profitable in a stagnating real economy, so investors turned to an increasingly speculative financial sector. This contributed to soaring share prices that bore no relation to the economic reality.

The Plaza Accord

In September 1985, the Plaza Accord between the USA, Japan, the Federal Republic of Germany,

France and the UK was signed at the Plaza Hotel in New York, marking the creation of the G5. This agreement aimed to stabilise the relative values of different currencies on the exchange market by using central banks to regulate the markets.

Indeed, the value of the dollar had risen by 44% since 1980, which led to a decline in the USA's trade balance and made American products less attractive on the global markets. The country's trade deficit rose from $112 billion in 1984 to $122 billion barely a year later. All of these contributory factors gradually accumulated and eventually destabilised the financial markets.

The Plaza Accord therefore prescribed intervention on the market in order to lower the value of the dollar in relation to the two strongest currencies of the time: the Deutsche Mark and the yen. These decisions paid off, particularly because currencies remained within certain exchange rate brackets: the dollar rate, which had shot up, stabilised again in just over two years. The value of the dollar dropped by 40% during this period, from nine to five francs and from 260 to 150 yen.

The Louvre Accord

In February 1987, the authorities wanted to stabilise the exchange situation and halt the decline in the value of the dollar resulting from the Plaza Accord. Consequently, the USA, Japan, Germany, France, the UK and Canada (all the countries of the G7 apart from Italy, which declined to sign the final agreement) came together to sign the Louvre Accord. In doing so, these six countries committed to more responsible monetary policies:

- the USA committed to reducing its expenses and getting its trade deficit under control;
- Japan was to curb its budget surplus;
- the UK agreed to reduce its public spending;
- France promised to reduce its government deficit.

Objectives were formulated using a bracket system consisting of target zones for currencies to aim for, which would have created the conditions for exchange rates to remain relatively stable.

Although the terms of the Accord, such as the particularly precise measures between the dollar and the yen, were kept secret in order to prevent speculation, the signatories were soon impacted by new external events.

The failure of the attempt

With German reunification underway, the thing the country feared above all was inflation, so it decided to raise its exchange rates to prevent this. Meanwhile, the dollar could not remain within the limits that had been set for it and continued to lose value in relation to the European currencies. Under this pressure, the main signatories soon abandoned their objectives, and the Louvre Accord was broken barely eight months after it was signed. This failure paved the way for the major disturbances which contributed to the crash in October 1987.

Japan was also entering a turbulent period at this time. Until this point, its economy had been strongly export-led, but the constant decline in the value of the dollar affected its savings in this currency. As a result, the price of equity investments and immovable property spiked, marking the beginning of a speculative bubble in Japan. When this bubble burst five years later, the country entered a decade of economic stagnation.

A TROUBLING GEOPOLITICAL CONTEXT

In terms of geopolitics, the Iran-Iraq War broke out in September 1980. Iraq, led by Saddam Hussein (President of Iraq, 1937-2006), feared Ayatollah Khomeini's (1902-1989) rise to power in Iran and sought to supplant its neighbour as the dominant power in the region. Consequently, Iraq attacked Iran in a large-scale assault that aimed to secure a fast, decisive victory. In the end, the war only came to end after eight years of bloody fighting.

Saddam painted the conflict as the defence of the Arab world in the face of Khomeini's Iranian Revolution, and as a result the USA, Great Britain, Italy and France provided Iraq with logistical support. This support was especially important as Iran and Iraq embarked on a "tanker war" that jeopardised the transportation of oil in the Persian Gulf, which was vital for the Western countries.

These events set the financial markets on edge: after American ships destroyed Iranian oil rigs in 1987 and 1988, the threat of retaliation by Iran hung over New York.

HOW THE CRISIS PLAYED OUT

After the successful Plaza Accord and the disappointing results of the Louvre Accord, the American economy took advantage of the almost 50% fall in the price of the dollar and entered an impressive growth phase.

This period of prosperity caused inflation to increase to such a point that some were worried that the Federal Reserve would intervene to correct interest rates. Indeed, interest rates had been rising briskly on the bond market since early 1987. As a result, American government bonds became significantly more attractive to financial operators than the stock market, leaving the stock market in danger of collapsing.

SHARES OR BONDS?

A share is a property title that represents a fraction of a company's share capital. When this company is listed on the stock market, its shares are then listed on the financial markets. Depending on the company's annual results, its shareholders can vote on a dividend.

A bond is not a property title but a debt instrument, meaning a proportion of the company's debt that it has to pay back, as it would with a bank. The value of the bond fluctuates over time, so while there is a possibility that it will increase, it could also decline.

Meanwhile, Germany took the unilateral decision to adjust its interest rates. This came as a shock to the American authorities, who were forced to let the dollar lose value in relation to the mark.

In October 1987, a series of events shook Wall Street and led to the crash.

ON WALL STREET

<u>HOW DOES THE STOCK EXCHANGE WORK?</u>

The stock exchange independently determines prices for the shares of the companies listed on it. This price varies over time because it depends on both supply (the propositions of the sellers) and demand (the propositions of the buyers).

Investors, meaning the people who want to acquire shares in one of the companies listed on the stock exchange, make their decision based on a technical analysis of the company and the price of its shares. Any event that is liable to have an effect on businesses, such as political announcements, economic news and the risk of conflicts is likely to affect prices of the shares listed on the stock exchange, by causing them to either increase or decrease.

On Wednesday 14 October 1987, the USA's trade deficit for August was announced, and left investors rattled because it was larger than expected (which meant that the country was living far beyond its means). At the same time, the American financial market began to dip, and this trend continued over the rest of the week. The dollar fell, interest rates rose and the downward pressure on share prices intensified, triggered by unusual activity from portfolio underwriters.

On Thursday 15 October 1987, the markets continued to decline. This can be attributed to the fact that pension funds and private investors became jumpy and preferred to take refuge on the bond market. Many shares were sold, and this rush to sell intensified in the final half-hour of the day.

On Friday 16 October 1987, the collapse of the market continued apace, and financial operators' anxiety spread. Traders then turned their attention to the futures market, meaning the market for the trading of shares that will not be paid and delivered until a fixed deadline in the future. On this market, contracts are sold to guard against any drop in stock value. Consequently, an ever-widening gap appeared between the values on the futures market and the corresponding reference values, which dragged share prices down. Traders capitalised on this gap to sell their shares and buy futures contracts instead.

The downward pressure on the American market intensified and by the end of Friday it was already experiencing one of the worst collapses in decades. The Dow Jones lost 108 points, equivalent to 4% of its value, over the course of the day. Such a drastic decline had never happened before.

An additional factor unexpectedly worsened the situation: the IT systems, which had never had to deal with an event like this before, continued automatically selling the shares they were monitoring, at such speed that there were even bottlenecks in the processing of orders. This further accelerated the fall in share prices.

The stock markets in Asia followed in the USA's footsteps. The Tokyo stock market lost 2.5% of its value, the Singapore stock market collapsed, and the Hong Kong stock market lost 11% of its value in a single day and had to be closed for the week. Europe's stock markets suffered the same fate: the Paris stock market lost 6% of its value in a single session, the Frankfurt stock market lost 7% and the London stock market lost 11%.

The following graphs illustrate the stock exchange indexes of the main countries affected from 1981 to 1988, shortly after the crash. The y-axis indicates the value of the stock exchange index.

New York

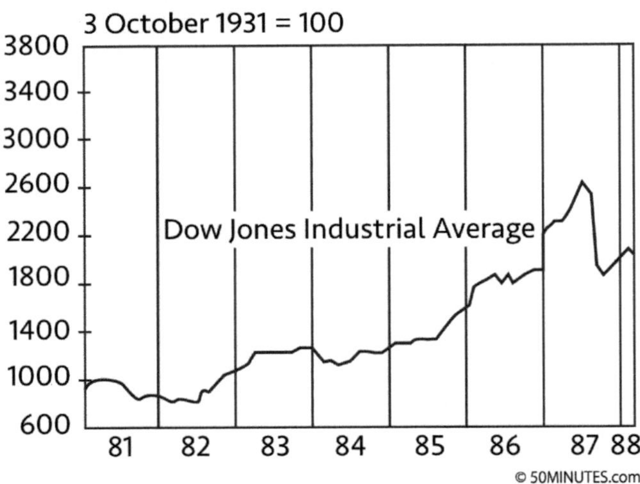

Tokyo

16 May 1949 = 176.21
32 000
27 500
23 000
18 500
14 000
9500
5000
Nikkei index
81
82
83
84
85
86
87
88
© 50MINUTES.com

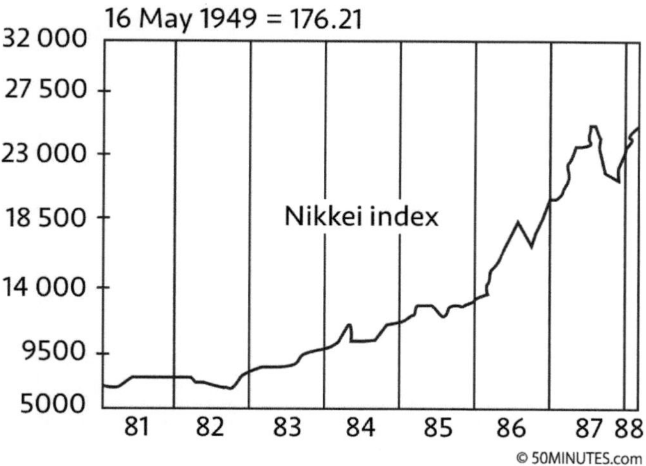

Paris

31 December 1981 = 100
500
425
350
275
200
125
50
CAC index
81
82
83
84
85
86
87 88
© 50MINUTES.com

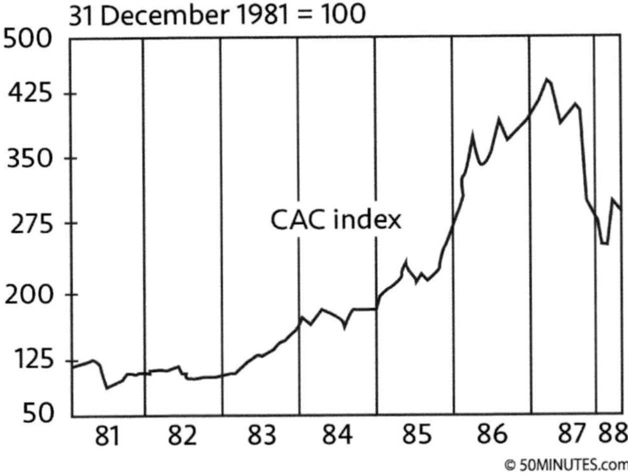

Frankfurt

December 1953 = 100
2900
2600
2300
2000
1700
1400
1100
800
500
81 82 83 84 85 86 87 88
Commerzbank AG
© 50MINUTES.com

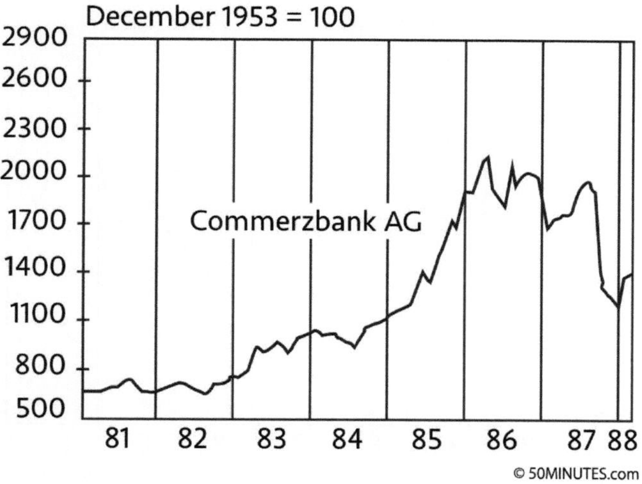

London

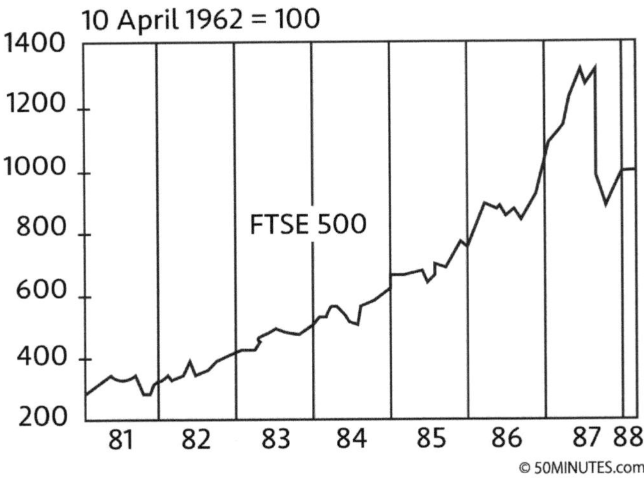

When the New York Stock Exchange opened on the morning of Monday 19 October 1987, all the operators were worried about the sizeable imbalance between the volumes of buying and selling orders. Many remained closed for the first hour, so initially the market only fell by a moderate amount. Of the 30 shares on the Dow Jones, 11 had still not been listed.

Conversely, the futures market began quoting and immediately collapsed. A discrepancy emerged between the value of stocks and the value of their futures contracts. When the shares were finally listed, they were sold for far less than the expected prices. Operators therefore bought futures contracts to compensate for their losses. This led to major confusion, and huge sales volumes were recorded. A few minutes later, the figures for America's trade deficit were published, signalling the collapse: Black Monday went down in history.

An hour after the start of the session, the index was down 100 points and panic rippled through the Dow Jones. There seemed to be no way of halting the collapse, and the authorities even considered closing the New York Stock Exchange. The record number of transactions disrupted and slowed down all the systems. It took more than an hour to execute orders, and by this point traders did not even know whether their orders had been processed or not. One major institution sensed that share prices were about to collapse and sold huge quantities of shares in large units. From 10 am onwards, it transferred 13 units of shares for $100 million each and for a total of $1.1 billion. Many traders tried to buy in the morning in order to combat the crisis by propping up share prices. However, when share prices collapsed, they could not pursue this approach.

By the end of the day, the market value of the Dow Jones had dropped by 22.6%. The index, which had been losing points since Wednesday, collapsed, losing 508 points to take it from 2246 to 1738. On Black Monday, $1000 billion simply evaporated as 600 million shares were traded, which had never happened before in the history of the Dow Jones. Even during the Wall Street Crash of 1929, the drop on Monday 28 October had only been 13%, just over half the drop recorded in 1987.

JUSTIFIED CONCERN

In his memoir *The Age of Turbulence: Adventures in a New World* (published in 2007), Alan Greenspan, who replaced Volcker as Chairman of the Federal Reserve in August 1987, discusses his worries on 19 October 1987. That morning, he thought about cancelling his trip to Dallas, but his advisors talked him out of it because they were worried that this change of schedule would increase operators' concern and make the situation even more volatile.

Greenspan writes that, when he got off the plane that evening and asked about the state of the stock market, he was told "five zero eight". At the time, he interpreted this as "5.8%", but it actually meant "508", the number of points that the Dow Jones had lost.

THE REST OF THE WORLD

When the main stock exchanges around the world opened that day, they all suffered rapid losses: 25% for Sydney, 15% for Tokyo, 12% for London and 10% for Paris. At the end of the month, when the results of all the operations between buyers and sellers were revealed in Paris, losses stood at 22%.

The closing of the American stock market on 19 October marked the end of Black Monday and allowed everyone involved to pick themselves up after a trying day. The following day, before the markets opened, the Federal Reserve published a statement by its chairman Alan Greenspan: "The Federal Reserve, consistent with its responsibilities as the Nation's central bank, affirmed today its readiness to serve as a source of liquidity to support the economic and financial system".

Bolstered by this show of support, and in spite of the sharp drops recorded by foreign stock markets overnight, things began to look up on the New York Stock Exchange. However, the situation was still precarious and some share listings remained closed. Later on in the afternoon, there was a sustained increase in share values, supported by the companies themselves in order to maintain demand for their shares.

It is clear that psychological factors, namely the panic and disorder that swept over the market and the herd instinct that guided operators' behaviour, had a decisive influence on this crisis. In this sense, the share values in themselves were not that significant, because many values had not been listed at the start of the session and it was impossible to obtain reliable information in this constantly shifting environment. The phenomenon was exacerbated by persistent rumours of market closure (which never came to pass in the end) and incomplete information. Some of the more opportunistic operators even tried to liquidate their positions at any cost.

In the end, the crisis made many operators realise that they had been reacting more to price fluctuations and their instincts than to real, pertinent information.

IMPACT

In the wake of Black Monday, the Federal Reserve's specific, proactive policy of supporting the banks prevented the disaster from spreading any further, unlike in 1929, and earned the institution the nickname of "lender of last resort". At the same time, it bought billions of dollars' worth of Treasury bonds in order to lower interest rates. President Reagan also took action at a political level, promising to work with the Democrats in order to reduce the USA's astronomical budgetary deficit.

These quick reactions meant that, in spite of the scale of the catastrophe, the first modern crash did not have a major impact on economic activity.

The US Congress learnt from these events, and in 1988 it asked the New York Stock Exchange to introduce short-circuiting mechanisms which would put a stop to trading once the market fell by over 10%.

The computer programmes used for financial operations also had to be modified. Their programming, which was still relatively untested, had contributed to this crisis by placing massive uncontrolled selling orders. Although computer trading cannot be held wholly responsible for the collapse of share prices during the crisis, it played an important role by systematically generating massive "stop" orders and yielding portfolio stakes. These factors need to be taken into account, even though non-computerised financial markets were also affected.

Subsequent events bore out the quick, decisive resolutions taken by the authorities of the financial world, led by Greenspan and the Federal Reserve, because the crisis was curbed one month after its sudden outbreak, and the markets enjoyed renewed growth. A number of lessons were learnt following the 1987 crisis:

- Respected authorities need to take public action to defend and support the market.
- Liquidity on the financial market must be made more dynamic. The Federal Reserve's decision to reduce interest rates allowed it to supply the banking system with liquidity, as

the institution immediately relaxed rules on the granting of loans.

- The Federal Reserve also encouraged operators on the market, in particular by granting loans to brokers so that they could keep working with their customers without too much difficulty.

These efforts made a major contribution to the recovery of a market that had been badly hit in the weeks following the crisis.

However, the crash was not entirely free of consequences: Black Monday caused astronomical losses, and 15 000 employees in the financial sector lost their jobs. The American bank L.F. Rothschild, which specialised in financial engineering and played a role in the IPOs of high-tech companies, did not recover from the crisis and went bankrupt in 1989. However, overall and taking into account the enormity of the losses, the real economy emerged relatively unscathed, and the American market continued to grow for another two years.

SUMMARY

- The Black Monday financial crisis in 1987 broke out suddenly and unexpectedly, but stemmed from global operators' inability to sustainably halt the continuing decline in the value of the dollar and stabilise the exchange rate, in spite of the Louvre Accord signed in Paris in 1987.
- While the Plaza Accord of 1985 had allowed the main global operators to come to an agreement and achieve their objective of stabilising the relative values of their currencies, the Louvre Accord of 1987, which aimed to stabilise the exchange situation and halt the ongoing decline in the value of the dollar, was powerless to stop the impending crisis.
- Although IT programmes for managing transactions, which had no safeguards at this time, were not directly responsible for the scope of the crisis, they worsened the situation, especially seeing as many orders were delayed for long periods, leaving traders uncertain.
- Although convincing explanations were put forward retrospectively, at the time the out-

break of the crisis was sudden and unexpected, which caused panic to spread to stock markets around the world. On Black Monday, the authorities even considered closing the New York Stock Exchange.

- Many operators did not obtain reliable data, opting to base their decisions on price fluctuations rather than any rational information. In the absence of information, herd instinct led to an irrational wave of panic which worsened the situation and allowed it to spiral out of control.
- The Dow Jones index collapsed, dropping by 22.6% from 2246 points to 1738. Over the course of a single day (19 October 1987), $1000 billion dollars evaporated as 600 million shares were traded.
- The effects of this collapse were felt on all the world's stock markets. The Tokyo and Singapore stock markets collapsed, while the Hong Kong stock exchange had to be closed for the week. Europe's stock markets faced the same fate, losing between 6% and 11% of their value in a single session.
- The day after the crisis, the Federal Reserve took robust, decisive action before the New

York Stock Exchange opened, providing banks with liquidity immediately and with no strings attached.

- Finally, although some feared the worst, companies were quick to bounce back from the crisis and the real economy emerged relatively unscathed. The American economy continued to grow, as if the crash had only been a slight bump in the road.

We want to hear from you!
Leave a comment on your online library
and share your favourite books on social media!

FURTHER READING

BIBLIOGRAPHY

- Bathelot, B. (2015) Définition : Pricing. *Définitions Marketing*. [Online]. [Accessed 28 September 2017]. Available from: <https://www.definitions-marketing.com/definition/pricing/>

- Carlson, M. (2007-2013) A Brief History of the 1987 Stock Market Crash with a Discussion of the Federal Reserve Response. *The Federal Reserve Board*. [Online]. [Accessed 28 September 2017]. Available from: <https://www.federalreserve.gov/pubs/feds/2007/200713/200713abs.html>

- Comparabourse. (No date) *Bulle spéculative*. [Online]. [Accessed 28 September 2017]. Available from: <http://www.comparabourse.fr/lexique/bulle-speculative.php>

- Signogne, P. ed. (1988) Le krash : avertissement sans frais. *Observations et diagnostics économiques : revue de l'OFCE*. 23(1), pp. 5-104. [Online]. [Accessed 28 September 2017]. Available from: <http://www.persee.fr/doc/ofce_0751-6614_1988_num_23_1_1133>

ADDITIONAL SOURCES

- Bozzo, A. (2007) Players Replay the Crash. *CNBC*. [Online]. [Accessed 28 September 2017]. Available from: <https://www.cnbc.com/id/21136884>

- Federal Reserve History. (No date) *Stock Market Crash of 1987*. [Online]. [Accessed 28 September 2017]. Available from: <https://www.federalreservehistory.org/essays/stock_market_crash_of_1987>

- Greenspan, A. (2008) *The Age of Turbulence: Adventure in a New World*. London: Penguin.